Calling All NEURONS!

How Reading and Spelling Happen

LORI C. JOSEPHSON

Calling All Neurons! How Reading and Spelling Happen

ISBN: 979-8-9882908-0-3 (Trade Paperback)
ISBN: 979-8-9882908-1-0 (eBook)
ISBN: 979-8-9882908-2-7 (Hard Cover)

Library of Congress Control Number: 2023910843

First Edition

Printed in U.S.A.

Edited by David Aretha; www.DavidAretha.com

Illustrated by Jamie Sale,
www.jamiesale-cartoonist.com

Cover Design and Interior Formatting by Becky's Graphic Design®, LLC
www.BeckysGraphicDesign.com

Video actors include Milo and Maxine M. and their mom, Sarah M.

Publisher's Cataloging-in-Publication data:

Names: Josephson, Lori, author. | Sale, Jamie, illustrator.
Title: Calling all neurons : how reading and spelling happen! / Lori Josephson; illustrated by Jamie Sale.
Description: Includes bibliographical references. | Lakewood Ranch, FL: Happy Hummingbird Press, 2024.
Identifiers: LCCN: 2023910843 | ISBN: 979-8-9882908-2-7 (hardcover) | 979-8-9882908-0-3 (paperback) | 979-8-9882908-1-0 (ebook)
Subjects: LCSH Reading (Elementary)--Juvenile literature. | Spelling ability--Juvenile literature. | Language arts (Elementary)--Juvenile literature. | Literacy--Juvenile literature. | Cognition in children--Juvenile literature. | Brain--Juvenile literature. | JUVENILE NONFICTION / Language Arts / General | JUVENILE NONFICTION / Science & Nature / Anatomy & Physiology
Classification: LCC LB1139.5.R43 J67 2023 | DDC 372.4--dc23

This book is dedicated to those I have taught, children, families and teachers alike, who taught me far more than I taught them.

It is often said that it is "better to give than to receive." I gave of myself so others were able to achieve the gift of literacy.

Table of Contents

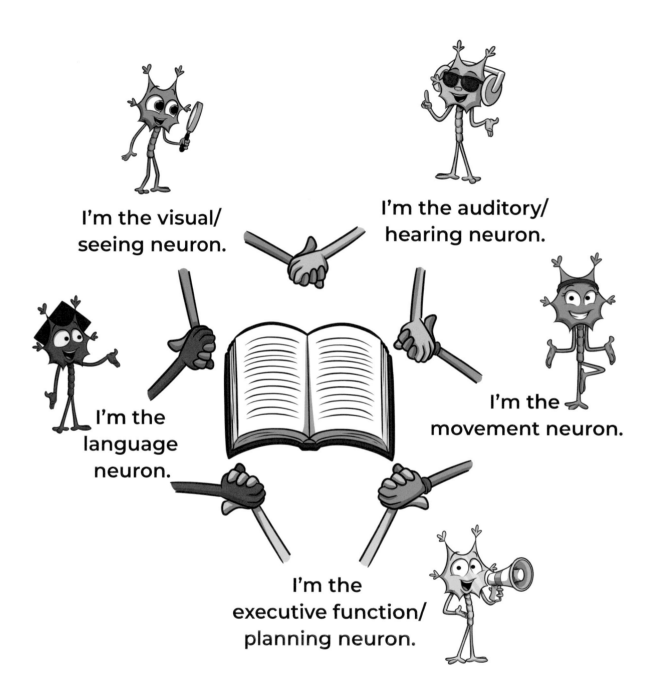

Guide to Reading This Book with Readers/Spellers in Training

I have had the desire to write a book **_for children_** _about how they learn to read and spell_ for many, many years! I am delighted to share this book with children, their parents, families, caregivers, and educators. Have a look at the About the Author section to learn more about me. Let's spend time on the book right now.

In asking children of all ages, as well as their teachers and parents, about "how they recall learning how to read," I got many blank stares and similar responses, including: "I don't know;" "My mom;" "I just learned the words;" "I practiced;" "I remember tracing the words;" "I didn't learn to read until the fifth grade and it was so embarrassing;" "I did it, but it was so hard for me," and so on.

Vast research using brain activation science (fMRI-functional magnetic resonance imaging), beginning in the early 1980s, has provided the opportunity to see what happens in the brain as children are learning language in terms of how it sounds, how to form the sounds, what the words mean, and then processing written words. My purpose in sharing this information is to foster an understanding of the process and provide ways to make this process easier to understand. My hope is that in sharing this literacy miracle in a concrete way, children, parents, families, caregivers, and educators can use the information to foster language and literacy from the moment a child is born.

Like all read-aloud books (or even if older children read this book independently), it is important to read and take as much time as needed to examine and discuss the concepts and illustrations. To be effective and fun, perhaps read one or two sections at a time with children, as well as briefly review previously read sections. As main characters of the book, neurons themselves take the stage, narrating the story and explaining the process of learning how to read and spell in a fun and upbeat way.

Rereading is something many children enjoy. Many children, as well as adult readers, will likely pick up information they may have missed the first time around.

Who will appreciate and learn from this book?

- Children on the "road to reading and spelling." In other words, the book is certainly appropriate for elementary school-aged children continuing on the reading path.

- Older readers/spellers who likely will find the information eye-opening and reassuring.

- Readers/spellers of any age (or adult readers) who have or had trouble learning to read, write, and spell. In my own experience teaching students struggling to attain literacy, all were receptive to information about how brain activation works, which served to improve motivation and validate their experiences.

- Busy parents and caregivers. Busy teachers. Need I say more? Knowing *what* children need to learn is important, but knowing *how* and *why* children learn is even better.

Enjoy the book!

Lori Josephson

Use Your Noodle:

Why Learn the Human Miracle That is Reading and Spelling?

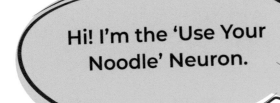

Hi! I'm the 'Use Your Noodle' Neuron.

"Reading Greetings!

What is a **neuron** [nü-rŏn]? Well, a neuron is a special type of cell.

Neurons receive information from your senses (eyes, ears, nose, mouth, hands) and send signals from one cell to another to make connections. These signals allow you to walk, talk, make memories, learn new information, and react to things around you. When neurons form connections with other neurons, the connections grow stronger. . . and faster.

Although no single neuron is in charge of how a person learns to read and spell, I am the 'Use your Noodle' Neuron who will be explaining this first part of the reading and spelling story to you.

The name 'Use your Noodle' has nothing to do with pasta. It's a way to say that a person learning to read and spell must **use their brain** and **think pretty hard** to figure out how to translate the words we see and hear into thoughts and ideas we can think about.

Why can't most of us remember how we learned to read or to spell?

Why is it harder for some humans to learn to read and spell than others in the language they learned to speak?

HOW READING AND SPELLING HAPPEN

What does the human brain need to do in order to make sense of:

- the language they hear?

- the sounds they hear in the spoken words?

- the lines, curves, dots, and squiggles they see?

- the shapes of the letters representing these sounds when they read?

- how to form the letters and sequence the letters when they spell words?

- and how to write the words they are thinking about for others to know their thoughts?"

"AS YOU READ THIS book, you will find out reading and spelling are two sides of the same coin. In other words, reading and spelling work together at the same time. Spelling helps readers become better readers. Reading helps writers become better spellers.

When a person **reads**, the task moves from **seeing** to **hearing**.

When a person **spells**, the task moves from **hearing** to **speaking**.

When a person **writes**, the task moves from **thinking about spelling** to **moving** as one writes or keyboards.

When a person reviews what has been **written**, the task moves from **writing** back to **seeing.**

THE FINAL GOAL OF being able to read and write is for the different parts of the brain (hearing, seeing, thinking, moving) to *work together* to help humans share meaning and ideas with each other. That's what reading and writing are all about. The stronger the connections of hearing, seeing, thinking, and moving, the more skilled the reader and speller becomes.

This book explains how our brains learn to read and spell. Kids, teachers, and even parents and caregivers need to know and may have questions about how reading and spelling "happen." You may ask these questions out loud, but sometimes you just think about them silently.

Researchers from many fields (brain, language, learning) have been studying how the human brain learns to make sense of the print we use to communicate. They know a lot about how our brains "work" and the jobs of the different neurons."

"Our brains have neurons for:

- auditory stimuli (hearing with our ears),

- language (making meaning from speech)

- motor stimuli (with a moving eye and a moving mouth/throat, hand writing with a utensil),

- visual stimuli (with eyes),

- memory and attention patterns necessary to become a reader and speller.

I'm using my listening ears

The explanation of the creation of a **literate brain** awaits! My fellow specialized neurons take the stage next to tell the story."

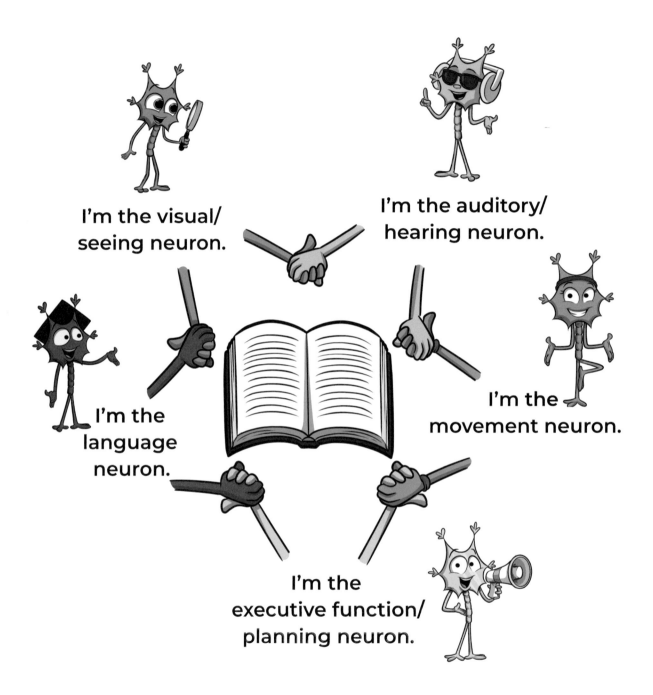

I'm the visual/ seeing neuron.

I'm the auditory/ hearing neuron.

I'm the language neuron.

I'm the movement neuron.

I'm the executive function/ planning neuron.

In the Beginning:

Before Reading/Spelling
We Speak

Reading Greetings from all of us! We are here to tell a story about how the brain learns to read and spell!

"EACH BABY'S BRAIN IS born with about **100 billion** neurons. That is a VERY big number and many more than other animals! We neurons allow people to see, hear, move, talk, learn, think, remember, feel emotions, and plan.

Even *before* babies are born, we neurons begin to connect and communicate with each other...a miracle of nature!

By the time babies are born, we neurons have migrated, or traveled, to different locations in the brain. Different neurons have different jobs. We neurons depend on each other to work together, just like a team works together. We work together to help babies grow to be toddlers and then to be children who can talk, walk, play, love, and understand what other people say."

FUN FACT

Unlike the majority of animals, people all over the world have been able to talk to each other for thousands of years. In fact, there are more than 5,000 languages spoken in the world.

"OTHER ANIMALS CAN MAKE sounds. A dog barks, a cat meows, a bird chirps, and a lion roars, but only human beings can put together sounds to make an enormous variety of words and share complex actions and ideas.

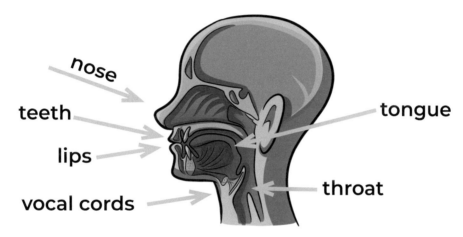

People use their lungs, throats, vocal cords, teeth, lips, noses, and tongues when they speak. People use their ears to hear and other parts of their brains to think and understand.

People did not use reading and writing to share ideas until about 6,000 years ago. When a person's thoughts are written down, that person and many other people can look back at them forever."

"**MOST BABIES BEGIN TO LEARN** language as soon as they are born and continue to learn every single day after that! Their parents look and talk to them all the time. Babies watch their parents' mouths and look at their eyes all the time too.

Babies LOVE to look at themselves in mirrors—that's because they are looking at their own faces and watching their own mouths moving to make sounds!

When babies make sounds like "ga, ga, ga" and "bu, bu, bu," they are practicing moving the muscles of their mouths and throats to make the speech sounds they hear.

It takes most babies nearly a year or more to start to put the sounds together to make words. And it takes at least another year for most babies to put words together to make sentences. Most babies and young children understand many more words and sentences than they can say themselves. No one has to teach babies how to talk—it is almost like magic that most people just 'do' naturally."

"I did it!"

"AS BABIES BECOME TODDLERS, they learn to understand and say more and more words and say longer sentences. They learn to walk, run, play, share, use the potty, and get in trouble! They also learn to show their feelings.

Some toddlers and preschool children even begin to **recognize letters of the alphabet** and **even their own names** when they see them!! They sing songs, listen to stories, pretend to read books, and even recognize special signs like a 'STOP' sign.

While all this is happening, little children's brains are grow-ing and learning all the time. Finally, a child's brain is ready to learn to read and spell! This happens for most children when they are between 5 and 7 or 8 years old. Every child needs an older adult, usually a teacher—or sometimes a parent or caregiver—to TEACH him or her HOW to read and spell using many of the different kinds of neurons in the brain. Neurons perform differ-ent tasks and create new literacy pathways and connections in the brain."

"**THE LETTERS OF THE** English alphabet look like shapes our brains already recognize around us like lines, curves, and circles.

Familiar shapes make the letters of our alphabet pretty easy to learn. These shapes can also make the letters a bit confusing to learn at the beginning since the letters are formed by changing the familiar shapes around in small ways.

A B C D E F G H

Many children think learning to read is about looking at and memorizing a lot of words. Reading and spelling are not only about *SEEING!* They are also about *LISTENING, THINKING, SPEAKING*, and *WRITING!* To become a reader and speller, a child must also pay close *ATTENTION* and *PRACTICE* a lot!! It is not a natural process like learning to talk. It takes a long time to become a great reader and speller. Researchers who study how our brains learn to read and spell tell us nearly all—95% of human beings—*CAN* do it, so read on!"

EYES (SEEING)

HAND (WRITING ON PAPER)

LANGUAGE (MAKING MEANING)

EARS (LISTENING)

"**LOOK AT THE HUMAN** brain again. Start with the red parts, where I hang out, located on both the left and right sides of the brain, which are called **hemispheres** [hĕm-ĭs-fērz]. Much of the work is done in the left hemisphere, but the right hemisphere also helps. These brain parts have long, scientific names sometimes named after the scientists who discovered them! Don't worry too much about what they are called, but do think about the jobs we neurons do!

Get ready! Here come some scientific terms!

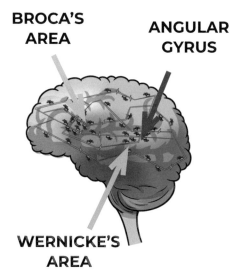

BROCA'S AREA

ANGULAR GYRUS

WERNICKE'S AREA

The **Angular Gyrus** [ăng-ū-ler jī-rŭs] is the place in the brain where the **Parietal** [pa-rī-ĕt-ŭl], **Temporal** [tĕm-por-ŭl], and **Occipital** [ŏks-ĭp-ĭt-ŭl] **Lobes** meet and work together to help people understand single words (things and ideas like 'mother,' 'five,' 'bed,' 'run,' 'love').

Wernicke's [wer-nĭck-ēz] **Area** in the **Temporal Lobe** works with the **Angular Gyrus** tucked way inside to help us figure out the meanings of several words grouped together and sentences. This helps us understand information and ideas (like 'clean your room,' 'watch out,' 'I love you').

Toward the front of the brain, my neurons in **Broca's** [brō-căhz] **Area** allow people to think about what they want to say using language. Future readers and spellers need to be able to understand words and how words are put together. For example, if you know that 'a bike' means one bike and that 'bikes' means more than one bike by adding the /s/ sound, that is **Broca's Area** at work!"

Hey, it's my turn to work. I am one of the neurons in the Motor Cortex and we are purple.

"**MOST PEOPLE WHO UNDERSTAND** language also speak the language before they learn to read the language. That's where we come in.

We neurons in the **Motor Cortex** in the **Frontal** [frŭn-tŭl] **Lobe** of the brain work with **Broca's Area** to be sure that the muscles in a person's face, mouth, tongue, nose, lips, and throat move in the right ways to make speech sounds and form words clearly.

HOW READING AND SPELLING HAPPEN

The **Cerebellum** [sĕ-rĕ-bĕl-ŭm], in the back of the brain, also works to do things like open and close a person's mouth so they can speak. In addition, the Cerebellum's neurons help humans learn to read and spell by coordinating eye movements, remembering things such as language and how to do things in a specific order, paying attention, and the timing of all of these activities."

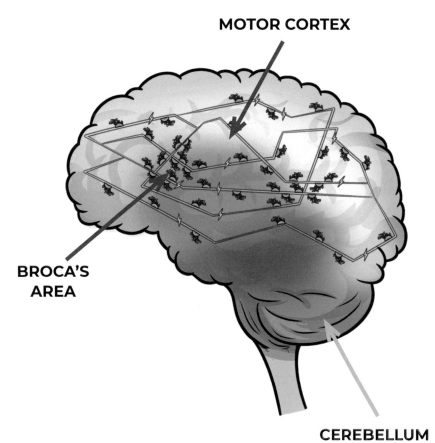

MOTOR CORTEX

BROCA'S AREA

CEREBELLUM

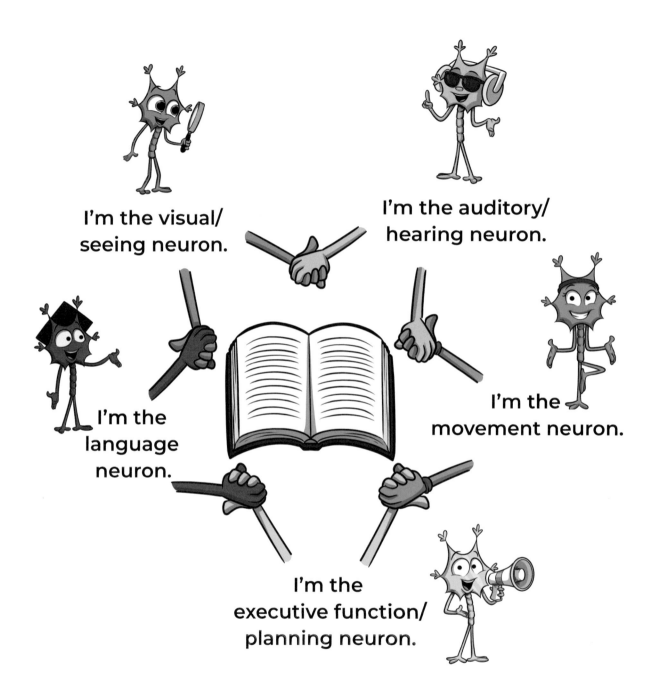

We Listen

I've really been waiting a long time for our part of the story. Our neurons are green!

"Our neurons are in the **Auditory** [au-dĭ-tor-ē] **Cortex** in the **Temporal** area of the brain—this area is all about hearing and listening. Sound travels through a person's ears and is sent right to us so that we can make sense of what we hear.

People need to hear many different parts of language to be able to learn to read and spell. They need to be able to tell where one word ends and the next word starts when they hear people talking.

Little babies learn to do this by listening to the *melody* of language when they hear their parents speak. Babies listen for changes in adults' voices going up and down, and they listen for when the adults take a pause or stop when speaking. It's a little like music!

Some people call this *baby talk*, but it really isn't. Parents and other adults are just speaking in a *big way* to emphasize the melody of language and speech sounds."

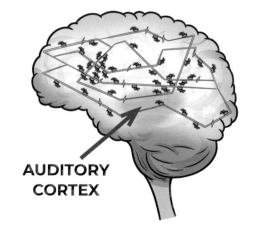

AUDITORY CORTEX

"LISTEN TO THIS SENTENCE:

I love you so much.

How many words does it have? That's right, 5 words.

How about this sentence:

I can't wait to see you today!

This sentence has 7 words, but little kids sometimes think it has 8 words because they still aren't sure if 'today' is 1 word or 2 words like 'to' and 'day.'

After a while, kids understand that 'today' is only 1 word even though each word part is also a word. This is because kids hear and pay attention to the word 'today' so many times. This is what 'practice' means.

Let's practice some more:

You can learn to read. How many words? **5**

The afternoons seem longer than the mornings. How many words? **7**

I like basketball better than baseball.

How many words? **6**

That one was tricky!"

Finally!! My turn to add! I'm blue. . .

"SOME KIDS UNDER- STAND HOW language works more easily than others, while some need practice for a longer time. People are all different and each person should get a chance to practice as much as is needed *for them*. A person who needs more practice than others does not mean that person is 'less smart' than a person who needs less practice.

When a person learns to read, that person will be able to SEE that words are separated by spaces when they are written. When a person talks, the spaces between words are invisible!!"

CAN YOU COUNT how many spaces are between the words in these sentences? Use your finger to count the spaces.

The__ball__is__red.
   1   2   3

How many spaces? **3**

I__like__vanilla__ ice__cream__best.
  1   2   3   4   5

How many spaces? **5**

How many words are in each sentence? Use your fingers to count the words below and listen too.

The ball is red.

How many words? **4**

I like vanilla ice cream best.

How many words? **6"**

I have a lot more to say . . .

"**BACK OFF, MY BLUE** neuron cousin! It's not your turn quite yet! I'm not done! We will come back to you soon!

There is a lot more kids need to learn from listening. As we neurons mentioned a bit ago, words can have 1, 2, 3, or even more parts. These parts are called **syllables** [sĭl-lŭ-bŭlz]. A syllable is a word or part of a word with a vowel sound you can hear, and most of the time it has consonant sounds too. When you make a vowel sound, your mouth is nearly always open, and you can hear a sound and feel movement, or vibration, on your throat.

Try it:

Say /ē/ like in 'eat' and feel your throat.

Say /ŏ/ like in 'octopus' and feel the bump on your throat where your vocal cords vibrate. This part of your throat is called the **larynx** [lă-rĭnks]."

eat

CALLING ALL NEURONS!

Of course, there's more to this . . .

"NOW HAVE AN ADULT blow up a balloon, but don't tie a knot at the end.

Hold the neck of the balloon and slowly let the air out. Feel the neck of the balloon while you are letting the air escape. . . that's what the vibration feels like on your vocal cords!

Pull the neck of the balloon wider and narrower and you will hear the different sounds—that's how your vocal cords work!"

Watch this quick video:
"How the Human Larynx Works Like a Balloon"

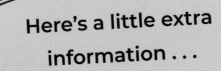

Here's a little extra information . . .

"SOMETIMES LONG WORDS HAVE more than 1 sound in each syllable, but each syllable *always* has at least 1 vowel sound.

Put your hand under your chin and say *me*.

How many times did you feel your chin drop?

That's right, 1 'chin drop,' so the word has 1 syllable.

Now put you hand under your chin and say *blanket*.

How many chin drops?

That's right, 2 chin drops, so the word has 2 syllables.

How many syllables are in your name?

Put your hand under your chin and count the number of chin drops.

You got this."

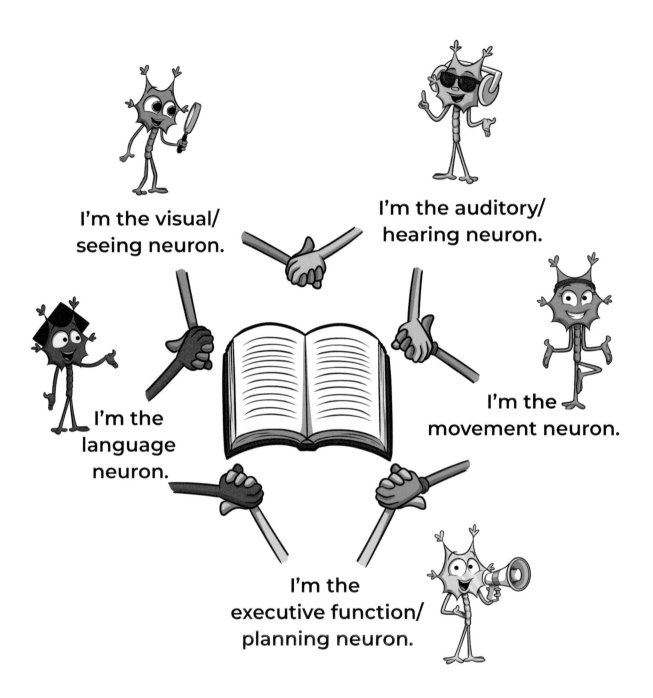

I'm the visual/ seeing neuron.

I'm the auditory/ hearing neuron.

I'm the language neuron.

I'm the movement neuron.

I'm the executive function/ planning neuron.

We Continue to Listen

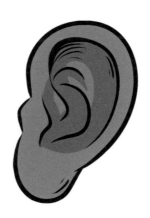

I have EVEN MORE
to add now . . .

"**ALL OF WHAT I** talked about before is called **phono-logical** [fŏ-nō-lŏj-ĭk-ŭl] **awareness**—that's a REALLY big word. But there is more to learn and practice!

Can you think of words that rhyme with *bat*? Most kids know a rhyme when they hear one and can also think of their own rhymes. 'Soon-to-be readers and spellers' must also be able to *hear the little bitty speech sounds* in each word.

Try it!

cat, sat, mat, hat

Do *cat* and *dog* rhyme? Nope!

How about *bat* and *cat*? Yes indeed!

When words rhyme, only the **first** *little bitty speech sound* is different. The other sounds in the words stay the same.

Can you name other words that rhyme with *bat*?

I can!! Some real words are: cat, sat, mat, hat

Silly, make-believe words that rhyme with 'bat' are: zat and jat

Learning about rhymes is easy for some 'soon-to-be readers and spellers,' but not for all. You can still learn to read even if rhyming is hard for you."

> There's even
> MORE . . .

"'SOON-TO-BE READERS AND SPELLERS' must also be able to hear the *differences* between speech sounds, to remember them in order, and to know how to move the sounds around in their heads."

FUN FACT

These speech sounds are called **phonemes** [fō nēmz]. English has 44 phonemes. Other languages have different numbers of phonemes and not every language has the same phonemes as English.

"SO LET'S USE THE word *bat*.

What's the beginning, or first, sound in *bat*? Yes, it's /b/.

What's the middle, or second, sound in *bat*? It's /ă/.

What's the final, or third, sound in *bat*? It's /t/.

When we put slanted lines around a letter like /t/, it represents the *sound* the letter makes us think of instead of the *name* of what the letter looks like.

My blue neuron cousins will explain in a minute!"

I'm still narrating . . .

"KIDS WHO ARE GETTING ready to learn to read and spell need to 'play with sounds' they hear every day so they get lots of practice.

Here are some 'word games' kids can work on when they are ready:

Say *bat*. What are the phonemes or speech sounds in *bat*?

Try it. That's right, it's /b/. . . /ă/. . . /t/!

Say *bat* and change the first phoneme to /k/. What's the new word?

Try it. That's right, it's *cat*!

Say /k/. . . /ă/. . . /t/. What word can we make from these phonemes?

You've got it!"

cat

Let me continue . . .

Watch this video to see examples of sound blending and segmenting.

"MAYBE A GROWNUP WILL say *bat* in slow motion, pausing after each sound like this: /b/. . . /ă/. . . /t/. A new or practicing student can listen and put those sounds together to make the word *bat*! This is called **sound blending**. Practice with blending will help make reading easier.

A new or practicing student can say the word *bat* and then take the word apart into its *little bitty speech sounds*. The reader would say /b/. . . /ă/. . . /t/. This is called **sound segmenting**. Practice with segmenting will help make spelling easier.

Here are some more words to practice: **dig   up   sock**

Reading researchers have found that it's best to practice these skills when the new or practicing student also sees the letters.

dig

WARNING! It is important to remember that 'b' = /b/ and not /bŭ/, and that 't' = /t/ and not /tŭ/. If the extra /ŭ/ is added to consonant sounds, it is much harder to blend sounds into real words or segment sounds into their correct spellings. The /ŭ/ is called a **schwa** [shwŏ] sound, and it looks like /ə/ in a dictionary."

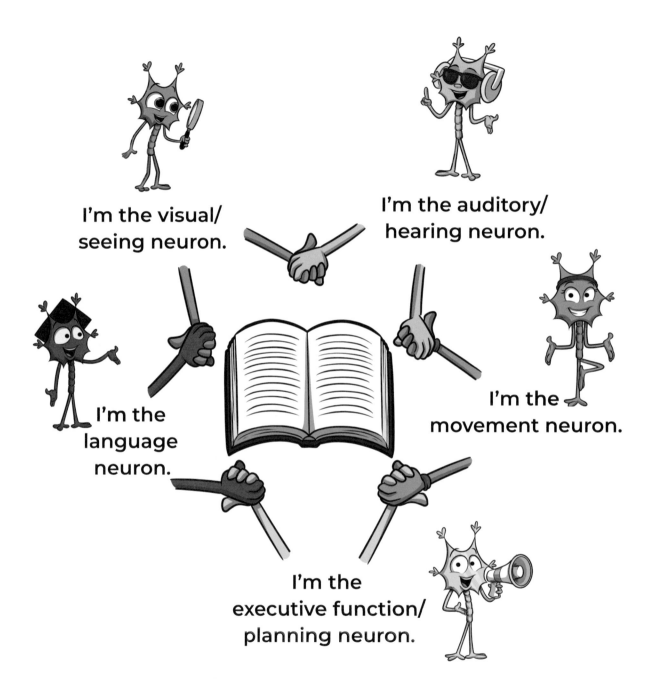

We See

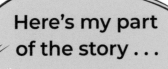

Here's my part of the story . . .

"**FINALLY, IT IS MY** turn—my neurons are in charge of what a reader sees! We are blue!

When beginning readers look at a word, their eyes send messages to the visual neurons in the **retina** [rĕt-ĭn-ŭ], which is a part of the actual eye. The retina's neurons send the word to the back of both sides of the brain in the **Occipital** [ŏk-sĭp-ĭt-ŭl] **Lobe** in the **Visual** [vĭzh-ŭ-ŭl] **Cortex**. Do not worry about these fancy names! Let me remind you these are the visual neurons. 'Visual' means 'what a brain sees.'

This is done SO very fast—in less time than it takes to 'blink an eye.' Did you know that skilled readers see 7 to 9 letters all at once, pausing for only fractions of a second? Skilled readers' brains pay attention to every letter in every word very quickly. It's amazing!"

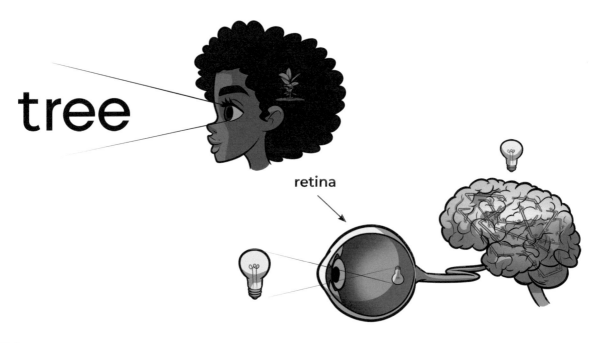

tree

retina

It's true, and I have EVEN MORE to add . . .

"**WE VISUAL NEURONS WORK** together to help with reading and spelling, but . . . we all have many different jobs and we like to hang out in our own spaces in human brains.

Some of us see single letters called **graphemes** [grăf-ēmz], one at a time. We can even recognize these letters in different sizes, designs, or **fonts**. A **font** is a particular size, shape, and style of a letter. No matter how different the letters may seem, they still share basic shapes of the individual letter readers recognize. And . . . we can recognize if the letters are uppercase or 'capital letters' and lowercase letters.

Some of us see groups of letters that go together a lot—that is called a 'pattern.' These are also called **graphemes** [grăf-ēmz]. These graphemes most often represent spellings of English **phonemes** (speech sounds). Examples of English letter patterns often appearing together are:

Aa Bb Cc
Aa Bb Cc

qu   In English, we never see a 'q' without a 'u' unless it is a name or a foreign word. We see 'qu' in words like 'quack,' 'quit,' and 'quiet.'

wh   In English, we usually see 'wh' at the beginnings of words, and for sure in question words like 'what,' 'when,' 'where,' and 'why.'

oy   In English, we usually see 'oy' at the ends of words like 'toy' and 'cowboy.'

tion   In English, we see 'tion' at the ends of words most often. We start seeing this pattern by the time readers and spellers are about 9 or 10 years old in words like 'nation' and 'motion.'"

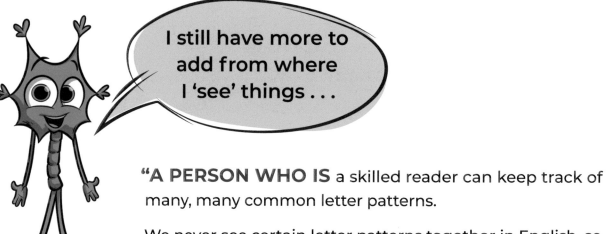

CALLING ALL NEURONS!

I still have more to add from where I 'see' things . . .

"A PERSON WHO IS a skilled reader can keep track of many, many common letter patterns.

We never see certain letter patterns together in English, so they 'look funny' to us and we neurons will almost ignore them. They may be letter patterns like:

zlmx   OR   **pfaj**

WE BLUE NEURONS GET SOOOO good at seeing some of the same words over and over again. Early readers or even kids who cannot yet read actually *remember many of the words* they see just by looking at them *right away.*

Some of these words are:

Your name!   My name is _____.

Names of the people in your family!

My parents' names are _____.

My sisters' and brothers' names are _____.

OR if you are older:

Names of family members:

Parents: _____ Siblings: _____

In school, you have seen many or even all of these words:

the   to   come   what   a   school   where   gym   lunch"

We Put the Code Together

"HERE'S WHERE READING AND spelling can get really 'tricky' because **ALL** of us neurons have to start *working together* to make *READING AND SPELLING HAPPEN!!!* This is the part of this story that is most complicated since human beings, remember, were not 'born' being able to read and spell.

When a reader is first learning to read and spell, the reader must be able to match sounds they **hear** to the letters of our alphabet they **see**. It's like learning a spectacular and special code!

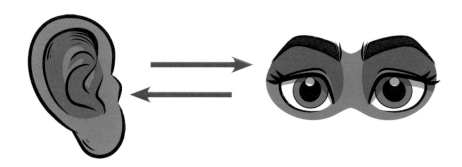

A B C D E F G H I J K L M N O P Q R S T U V W X Y Z

The English language has 44 phonemes or sounds.

The English alphabet has 26 letters.

These 26 letters can be put together to represent or stand for all 44 sounds (or phonemes) making up the English language."

There are more phonemes in English than letters, so some of the 26 letters have more than one job and stand for more than 1 sound or phoneme since 44 > 26.

FUN FACT
These 26 letters can be used to make all the words in English—that's over 1,000,000!

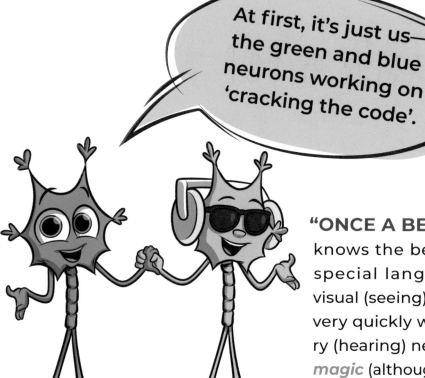

At first, it's just us— the green and blue neurons working on 'cracking the code'.

"ONCE A BEGINNING STUDENT knows the beginning parts of this special language code, the blue visual (seeing) neurons start working very quickly with their green auditory (hearing) neuron cousins. And *like magic* (although it's not really magic!!), a beginning reader and speller will be able to read and spell words like:

bat   cut   dog

At first, reading and spelling these words will be slow because a new reader must:

1. look at each letter of the word when reading OR listen for each sound in the word.

2. match each letter with each sound when reading OR write each letter representing each sound when spelling, so our purple 'motor' neurons get to work by writing the letters. *Writing the letters helps new readers learn the code more easily and quickly.*

3. put all the sounds together to make a word if reading. It looks like this:

bat = /b/. . ./ă/. . ./t/ = /bat/

OR

write 'b' 'a' 't' in order of the sounds they hear to represent the word if spelling like this:

b a t

Most new readers and spellers will catch on to *the special code* pretty easily and be able to **decode** or *sound out* (match one letter at a time to its sound) a little bit faster with enough practice until they can look at the word and just say *bat*."

How do all the words fit into people's brains?

"IF NEW READERS PRACTICE spelling at the same time, both spelling and reading will get easier and faster too.

The more a new reader and speller practices, the more words the new reader and speller will be able to read and spell. After enough practice, the new reader's brain will have 'taken a snapshot' of some of the words and they will be stored in the brain. This is called **automaticity** [au-tō-mă-tĭs-ĭ-tē]. This is AMAZING, right???

CALLING ALL NEURONS!

Most readers and spellers who practice enough will be able to read without sounding out each letter and spell without listening for each sound. Reading and spelling become automatic and these recognized words are known as *sight words*. All words want to be sight words, no matter their letter patterns.

As readers become more skilled and fluent, they use a process called **orthographic mapping** [or-thō-gră-fĭk] since every word has 3 forms—its *sounds* (phonemes), its *spelling* (orthography—this is a fancy word for 'spelling'), AND its *meaning*. Through orthographic mapping, readers use the oral language processing part of their brain, our red neuron cousins, to *map* (connect) the *sounds* (phonemes) of *words they already know* to the letters (the spellings) in a word. This is the process which allows readers to permanently store the connected sounds and letters of words (along with their meanings) as instantly recognizable words, described as 'sight vocabulary' or 'sight words.'"

/s/ /t/ /o/ /p/

stop

/d/ /i/ /g/

dig

/b/ /a/ /t/

bat

We are back to me, the blue visual neuron.

"HERE IS A SENTENCE a reader may see with this picture near it:

A dog sat on a bed.

First, imagine we blue visual neurons first 'see' groups of letters, and then send this information to the **Occipital Lobe** in the back of the brain on the left side.

Then, the blue visual neurons send information to my green hearing neuron cousins in the **Temporal Area**. We send the information by touching the ends of our neurons to each other. These endpoints are called **dendrites** [děn-drīts], which are attached to **axons** [ăks-ŏnz]. The axons are long, slender growths emerging from the center of nerve cells. The signals are both electrical and chemical, and are sent faster than you can read this sentence or send an email. Do you believe people have electricity in their brains?"

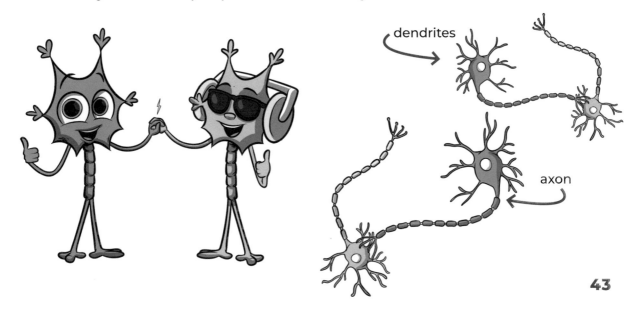

dendrites

axon

CALLING ALL NEURONS!

"FOR READERS *JUST LEARNING* to how to read, the blue and green neurons work on the sentence this way:

1. The reader will *look at each word* going from *left* → *right*.

2. Most children learning to read have learned the word **'a'** just by seeing it so often.

3. The reader will then look at the word **'dog'** and say **/d/ /ŏ/ /g/**, and then blend these 3 sounds to then say **'dog.'**

4. Next, the reader will look at the word **'sat'** and say **/s/ /ă/ /t/**, blending these 3 sounds to then say **'sat.'**

5. Then, the reader will look at the word **'on'** and say **/ŏ/ /n/**, blending these 2 sounds to then say **'on.'**

6. And then, the reader will look at the word **'bed'** and say **/b/ /ĕ/ /d/**, blending these 3 sounds to then say **'bed.'**

Finally, a beginning reader who is *on the way to skilled, fluent reading* will reread the sentence as:

A dog   sat on a bed.

The picture of the dog sitting on the bed should <u>**not**</u> be used to help a new reader *read* the sentence. A beginning reader **<u>needs to look at each word and each letter in each word</u>** in order to truly *read* the sentence. The pictures are only there to **<u>aid the new reader as a way to double check for understanding of the sentence</u>**. Looking at the pictures is not a good way to read the sentence.

Our red language neuron cousins will explain soon.

As you likely can tell by now, learning to read and spell is a bit complicated."

Okay, we seeing, hearing and moving neurons have something to add to the group . . .

"AND IF READERS ARE using their fingers to touch the words when reading out loud, the purple neurons in charge of moving get into the act since we control mouth and hand movements. Some readers even move their mouths and 'whisper read' when they read 'silently!'

Once new readers and spellers practice and become better at reading and spelling, they have learned many, many, many short words and can usually recognize and spell them very quickly. But then . . . they start reading books that have LONGER words they have NEVER seen before.

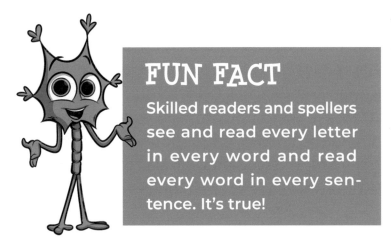

FUN FACT

Skilled readers and spellers see and read every letter in every word and read every word in every sentence. It's true!

Then all of us—the blue, green, purple, and even the red neurons—really have to get to work!"

"TAKE A LOOK AT this sentence:

The children traveled to a cabin in Wisconsin with Mom.

Again, the reader will probably recognize the words 'the,' 'to,' 'a,' 'in,' and 'Mom' very quickly, but when they get to 'children,' 'traveled,' 'cabin,' and 'Wisconsin,' that's a different story!! The words seem to have SO many letters!"

Continuing on . . .

"THE READER WILL LOOK at 'children' first and we blue visual neurons will get to work. We will separate the word into syllables, so the reader will think about the word 'children' as:

chil   dren

Why would a reader and speller do this? Because . . . the student had a teacher or another adult who taught that reader HOW to separate longer words into smaller parts, or syllables. Plus, many readers will learn to quickly recognize frequently occurring letter patterns making up common word parts or syllables. Most students can then read the smaller parts more quickly and put them together to form the longer word. The students will also be able to spell these words syllable by syllable until spelling becomes quicker, too.

We blue and green neurons must work together to match the letters to the sounds AND the sounds to the letters very quickly. That's because these readers know many letter and sound patterns (more slowly for some students, though) for each syllable. We THEN put the syllables together to read the longer words.

How do we neurons know how to separate these long words into syllables? Let me tell you, it takes a lot of work and practice most of the time. We neurons have to learn about several common ENGLISH SYLLABLE PATTERNS.

Many students, parents, and even teachers are not familiar with English Syllable Patterns. Even if skilled readers haven't been directly taught this, many of these readers just "know" and use this information when they read and spell."

> What ARE English Syllable Patterns?

> We're not finished yet.

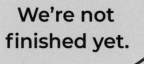

"THE MOST COMMON SYLLABLE PATTERNS are explained on pages 86 and 87 of this book, so everyone can look more carefully. Let us just say that skilled readers will know to divide a word like

Wisconsin into /wĭs/ /kŏn/ /sĭn/.

Skilled readers and spellers would never look at *Wisconsin* and try to read it this way:

/w/ /ĭ/ /s/ /k/ /ŏ/ /n/ /s/ /ĭ/ /n/

or spell it by separating it into each sound and then writing the letter representing each phoneme."

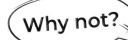

Why not?

"LET ME, THE GREEN neuron, answer that question. We green neurons can't remember 9 sounds in order—that's WAY too many sounds for us!

We can handle the 3 chunks or syllables much more easily than all of those sounds! By the time we would get to the last 3 sounds, we would have forgotten the ones at the beginning of the word!"

"HOW QUICKLY A PERSON learns to read and spell depends on each reader and speller. Some readers and spellers learn LOTS of words very easily, and for other readers and spellers, it takes A LOT more PRACTICE. People who struggle to learn to read and spell, even if they have a teacher who knows how to teach reading and spelling well, may have dyslexia.

What was that again?

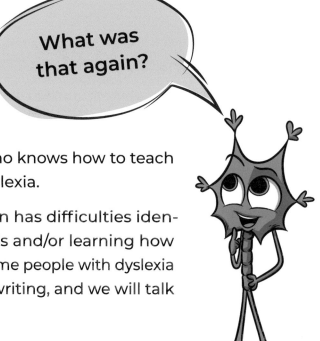

The person who has dyslexia most often has difficulties identifying separate speech sounds in words and/or learning how letters represent these speech sounds. Some people with dyslexia also have difficulty with the act of handwriting, and we will talk about that later on in the book.

We keep working as a team . . .

Having dyslexia can make school success more challenging, but it doesn't have to be this way if the person has a desire to learn and is willing to keep practicing with the support of teachers, families, and caregivers. Sometimes, students with dyslexia have extra time to take tests or listen to audiobooks.

If you suspect you or someone you know may have dyslexia, feeling comfortable enough to speak to an adult about your suspicions is 'a must.' The sooner people with dyslexia get help and support, the better off these people will be."

FUN FACT

As many as 15-20% of the population as a whole have symptoms of dyslexia including slow or inaccurate reading, poor spelling, poor writing, or mixing up similar words. Dyslexia occurs in people of all backgrounds and intellectual levels. Many people believe dyslexia has to do with seeing letters/words backwards, but this is untrue. Rather, dyslexia's causes have to do with differences in how the brain develops and functions. Dyslexia tends to run in families, which means that if a parent or other relative has dyslexia, a younger relative is more likely to have dyslexia too. If you want to learn more about dyslexia, scan the QR code.

Take a dyslexia self-assessment test - it comes right up on the website when you scan the QR Code.

"SO, BY THE TIME *most readers and spellers* are in second or third grade, we visual neurons have *stored or saved* thousands of words and many letter patterns in the **Occipital Lobe** of the brain. We recognize them so fast that we don't use our green auditory neuron cousins when reading and spelling except when we are trying to figure out new and longer words."

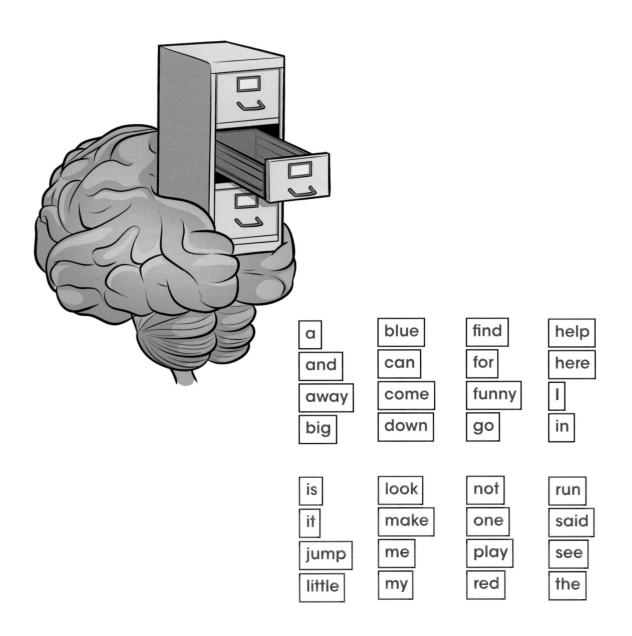

We Practice the Code A LOT!

"**NOW WE ARE INCLUDING** our purple 'moving' neurons along with us.

And there's another very important part of becoming a reader!

If new readers read words only one at a time, like this:

A   dog   sat   on   the   bed.

Instead of :

A dog   sat on the bed. OR *A dog sat   on the bed.*"

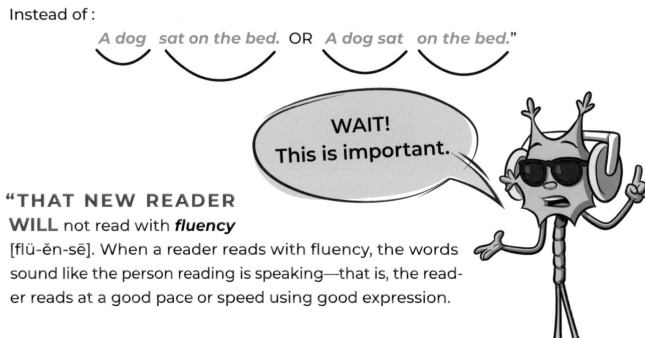

"**THAT NEW READER WILL** not read with *fluency* [flü-ĕn-sē]. When a reader reads with fluency, the words sound like the person reading is speaking—that is, the reader reads at a good pace or speed using good expression.

If a reader reads one word at a time, a most unfortunate thing will happen! That new or beginning reader will forget the beginning of the sentence by the time they get to the end of it!

Just like if a hula-hoop spins too slowly or stops, it will fall down."

We visual and auditory neurons have more to say . . .

"**OH NO! ALL THAT** work for nothing! The new reader will not have any idea of what the sentence means! These readers will not imagine or think of a dog sitting on a bed in their minds like they should.

And if the book has a picture of a dog on a bed, these readers may stop looking at the words and just use the picture to figure out the words, *which is not what reading is about at all*.

Pretty soon, only words will be on many of the pages and these readers won't have pictures to look at anymore. Skilled readers must know the special code when we blue and green neurons work together."

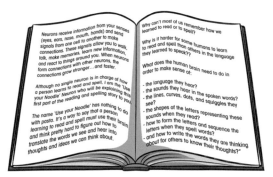

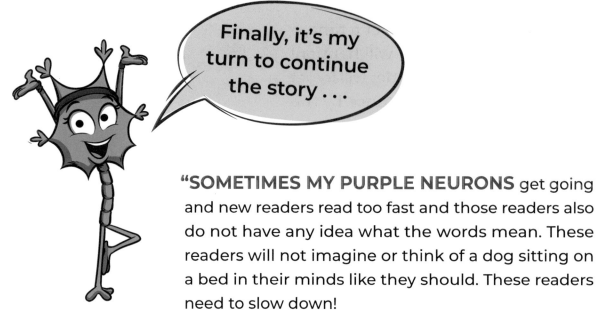

Finally, it's my turn to continue the story . . .

"**SOMETIMES MY PURPLE NEURONS** get going and new readers read too fast and those readers also do not have any idea what the words mean. These readers will not imagine or think of a dog sitting on a bed in their minds like they should. These readers need to slow down!

As we mentioned, skilled readers read the words *just like they are talking*. These readers will stop at the ends of sentences when they see periods, and stop just a little, *pausing* when they see commas and also when the words create a part of the 'picture' forming in their minds. Oops, I'll let my red language neuron cousins take over to explain that soon!"

Let me add a little more . . .

"**IF A READER READS** the sentence quickly without separating it into phrases that mean something, the reader may have little to no understanding of what they read. The reader may be confused. It is important to read with **prosody** [prŏz-ō-dē], which means reading with phrasing and expression, just as one would speak.

Later on, a reader may read a sentence like this with fluency:

A dog sat on the bed, snuggled with the family, and went to sleep.

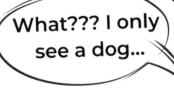

What??? I only see a dog...

Look at the 3 pictures below, which demonstrate what I mean about adding to the picture in the reader's mind."

"NEW READERS SHOULD PRACTICE reading *like they talk* every day! Reading out loud is a great way to practice! They need to practice in school and at home. It's okay to practice reading the same words, sentences, and stories a few times. This practice really helps. It is just like going to soccer, basketball, or piano practice every week.

In reality, ALL of the neurons play a role when reading becomes fluent and automatic. The blue visual neurons contribute to reading words automatically, while the green neurons help to decode words efficiently. The purple motor neurons assist with smooth eye movements, while the red language neurons help to quickly recognize the meanings of individual words, as well as aid in understanding phrases, sentences, paragraphs, and pages of what has been read. Finally, the golden 'Use Your Noodle' neurons come into play to keep the reader paying attention to the task at hand."

We Understand the Printed Text

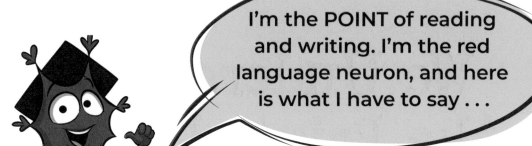

I'm the POINT of reading and writing. I'm the red language neuron, and here is what I have to say . . .

"WAIT, ONE MORE THING! New readers do not become skilled readers unless I get back into the picture in a big way!

While all of this activity is happening in the brain, the seeing, hearing, and moving neurons must check in with ME!

Again, so fast, I sort the information already stored in my area of the brain to make connections to the new visual and sound information. If the reader sees and says the word 'bat,' I *immediately* help the reader to picture all the different kinds of *bats*!"

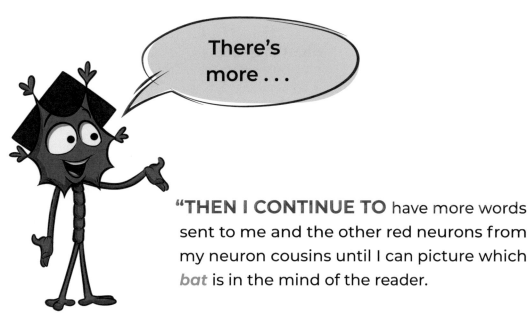

There's more . . .

"**THEN I CONTINUE TO** have more words sent to me and the other red neurons from my neuron cousins until I can picture which *bat* is in the mind of the reader.

So if the sentence is:
The bat struck the ball so hard that it broke,
the reader would picture:

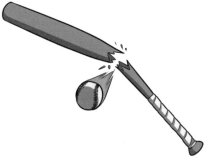

But if the sentence is:
We see a bat flying overhead in my yard every evening,
the reader would picture:"

Moving on . . .

"ONCE THE READER HAS the correct picture in their mind, thanks to us language neurons, a skilled reader would realize that the other sentences coming after these sentences would be about one of two things: either a baseball game or the nocturnal animal flying overhead who may live in caves or in trees and comes out at night.

This information helps us *predict more about the words* sent in my direction. This helps to create not only one picture in a reader's mind, but the entire story of what is read.

When skilled readers know a lot about what they are reading, it helps the visual and auditory neurons more easily *predict what the words will be* because they already are familiar with the *vocabulary* that will likely be used. This results in improving the reader's *background knowledge* about whatever topic or story is read."

> Let me tell you about the fast-moving 'neuron highways' connecting me with my blue, green, and purple neuron cousins . . .

"WE NEURONS CONSTANTLY SEND information back and forth to each other when all systems are working! The more a reader reads, the more the reader's vocabulary will grow, and the more about the world they will know and use when reading. One other thing: Listening to books also helps readers learn vocabulary and increase background knowledge.

Also, the better the readers get at knowing which *patterns of words go together* to help create a picture in their minds, the easier reading becomes.

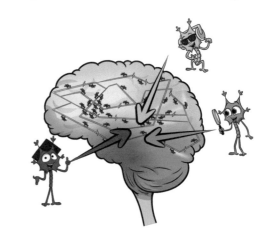

For example:

will be going and doing   OR

will have fun and eat candy   OR

will do the dishes and his homework

These all mean something that happens in the future, but hasn't happened quite yet. Maybe tomorrow, the day after that, or after that!"

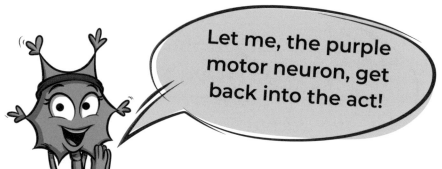

Let me, the purple motor neuron, get back into the act!

"**LIKE I SAID BEFORE,** if a reader reads out loud, then I get involved too!

Sometimes when a reader reads out loud, it makes it harder for the reader to get to my red language neuron cousins, but not always. It is very important for readers to realize when they do not understand what they read. This is called **metacognition** [mĕt-ŭ-cŏg-nĭ-shŭn]. When readers realize they do not understand, readers really need to stop:

- to read the sentence or paragraph again

- to figure out the words they are stuck on

- to ask someone for help

It's not a good idea to keep going, skip words, or just look at pictures. It is best to realize when unsure and do something about it to solve the problem!"

By the way, that is great advice for any type of problem!

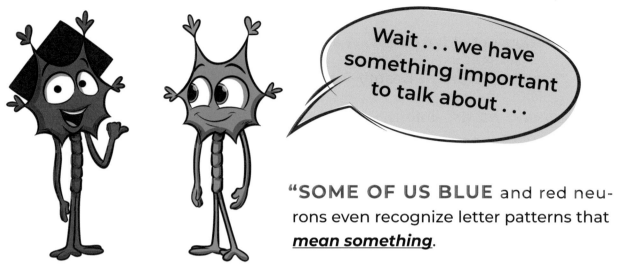

Wait . . . we have something important to talk about . . .

"SOME OF US BLUE and red neurons even recognize letter patterns that ***mean something***.

Letters or groups of letters sometimes appearing at the ends of words are called ***suffixes*** [sŭf-ĭks-ĕz].

A suffix can tell the reader:

- *when* something happens. The word *plant* means doing something now, but *planted* means it already happened in the past.

plant

planted

- *the number* of items. Remember *bike* means 1 bike, but *bikes* means more than 1 bike.

bike

bikes

When readers get older, *suffixes* can also tell or signal to a reader:

- *describing words*   beauty → beautiful = full of beauty

- *naming words*   inform → information = the knowledge someone is sharing

There are many, many suffixes to learn about in English and this takes a lot of time and practice. Readers will learn about these as their reading improves."

"*PREFIXES* [PRĒ-FĬX-ĔZ] ARE PARTS of words readers see at the beginnings of words—and they mean something too! Prefixes like these help readers understand the meanings of new words.

'**ex**' means 'out,' so words like **ex**it and **ex**hale all have something to do with going 'out.'

'**in**' can mean two things:

'not' in words like **in**complete (not complete), **in**experience (not having experience).

'in' in words like **in**hale (take in), but most often, 'in' means 'not.'"

Let's continue . . .

exit   **in**complete   **in**experience   **in**hale   **ex**hale

"PARTS OF WORDS THAT good readers see often and recognize appear in many words and have meanings, too! These are called *roots* (sometimes these word parts are referred to as *bases*)."

Also . . .

trans = across

photo = light

port = carry

struct = build

"WORDS COMING FROM LATIN (a language used in Europe long ago) often have prefixes, roots, and suffixes. Words coming from Greek (language coming from Greece) often have what are called 'combined forms,' so 2 roots can be put together to form more complicated words. These words are often English's scientific and mathematical words. Take a look at these words.

transport = carry across

photosynthesis = make energy with light

Knowing about roots helps students understand even more vocabulary, which will make them better readers! . This is called **morphology** [mor-fŏl-ō-gē].

Practicing *spelling* prefixes, suffixes, and roots also helps **both** reading and spelling get even faster and better."

FUN FACT

English words come from many other older languages.

We have one last thing to explain . . .

"KNOWING PUNCTUATION HELPS READERS, too!

For example:

> **?** means asking a question.
>
> **.** means making a statement.
>
> **"   "** means someone in the story is talking or the writer is using someone else's words—these are called quotation marks!
>
> **(   )** parentheses [pŭ-rĕn-thŭ-sēz] tell the reader something is added.

It is good for readers to know the meanings of various symbols used in English to help them understand other things besides words! These are just a few of the symbols appearing in books in addition to words.

\#   \$ %   &   @   !   { }

CALLING ALL NEURONS!

Using punctuation helps convey your own ideas when:

- writing a story

- writing a report

- answering questions on tests

- writing a note to someone in your family

Using punctuation makes it easier for whoever reads what you wrote to understand your thoughts and ideas.

Not using punctuation can cause a lot of confusion!"

She moves, swings, and slides.

She moves swings and slides.

We Move

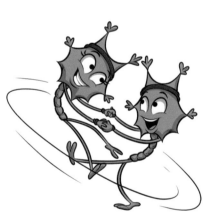

I'm back in the act for one pretty important thing.

"I BET SOME READERS and writers wonder why their teacher makes them hold the pencil the right way and practice handwriting.

We purple motor neurons help bodies move in the most efficient or quickest ways to get their jobs done. The parts of the hands that hold a pencil (thumb, index, and middle—sometimes ring finger) have lots of motor neurons, which send messages back to our blue, green, and red cousins! At first, writing is slow, but usually becomes very quick!

So, when a new reader and speller learns to form the letters of the alphabet or spell words, we purple neurons help the other parts of the brain to remember the sounds the letters stand for, what the letters look like, how to spell words, and even what the words mean when reading. When readers write, forming letters by hand helps them to learn to be a skilled reader and speller more quickly."

"**IF READERS HOLD THE** pencil using a fist or wrapping a thumb around the other fingers, we purple neurons get so tired, and then the writers also get so tired and sometimes don't want to write as much as they should. This makes learning to read, write, and spell much harder. Do you know anyone like this?

These days, it is important for skilled readers and writers to be able to keyboard too. And that also takes effort and muscle power. It is not a good idea to keyboard using only one or two fingers because that will also take too long to get the job done."

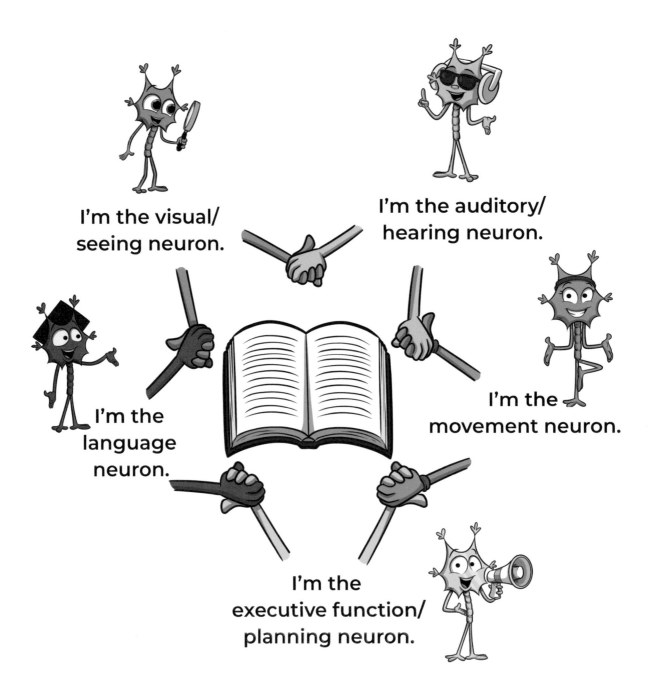

I'm the visual/
seeing neuron.

I'm the auditory/
hearing neuron.

I'm the
language
neuron.

I'm the
movement neuron.

I'm the
executive function/
planning neuron.

We Pay Attention and Keep Trying!

Don't forget about me—I'm one of the neurons in the **Frontal Lobe.** I am really, really important. Let me tell you why . . .

My neurons work right in front of the brain—we are behind a reader's forehead!

"**OUR NEURONS WORK IN** the largest part of a human being's brain, and this part of the brain is much larger than in other animals. That is why humans have oral (spoken) *and* written language—so humans can share information in ways animals cannot."

FUN FACT

Scientists have discovered that the Frontal Lobe of the brain is the very last one to finish growing. This part of the brain keeps developing until humans are between 25 and 30 years old!

> Let me fill you in on more details . . .

"MY NEURONS ARE IN charge of:

- **Planning and Organizing** – Our neurons control how our bodies move; steps to follow to complete a task like making a sandwich, taking a shower, or getting ready to learn at school.

- **Concentration, Paying Attention, and Motivation** – As humans get older, they are able to pay attention for longer amounts of time. Motivation is the desire to want to think about and work to finish a task or job.

- **Solving Problems** – We help human beings think about different ways to deal with problems big and small, and knowing the difference between right and wrong.

- **Working Memory** – Humans use working memory in order to *remember and work with* the information coming to and from our other neuron cousins.

- **Personality, Reactions, Emotions, and Feelings** – Humans' reactions to 'happenings' develop in appropriate ways so they get along with others the best they can. Remember, very young children start to cry when they are upset because they have not yet developed better ways to react to 'happenings'.

Think of my neurons as *running the show* or *conducting an orchestra*! We need language to make our golden neurons work well."

"**IN THE END, WE** Frontal Lobe neurons are the ones in charge of all learning. If we don't do our jobs well, our neuron cousins will not work as well as they could either.

It's important for '*soon-to-be*' readers and spellers, '*working-on-it*' readers and spellers, and even '*skilled*' readers and spellers to know all of this good stuff about how human brains work.

It is important to get enough rest, and feed the body healthy foods so that we neurons in the brain can work at our best and at top speed.

A human's brain is not a muscle, but it can work like a muscle. The more a human being uses their brain, the stronger it gets. The more practice a person actually spends reading, spelling, and writing, the better the reading, spelling, and writing gets most of the time.

Keep practicing! Learning to read, write, and spell takes a long time—usually several years. The more you read, write, and spell, the better you get at it. Many adults even say that they become better readers, writers, and spellers with every word, book, or newspaper they read."

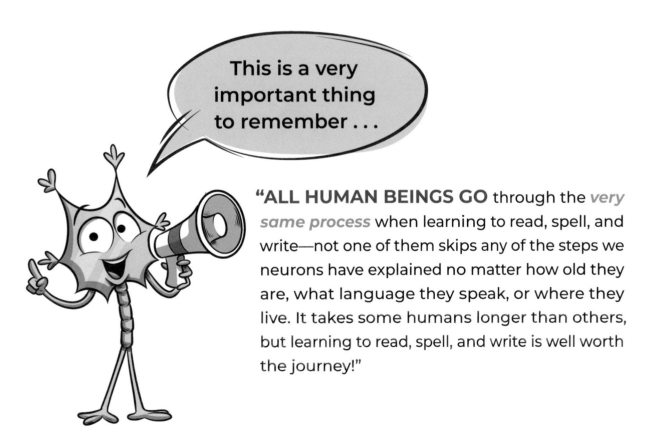

This is a very important thing to remember . . .

"**ALL HUMAN BEINGS GO** through the *very same process* when learning to read, spell, and write—not one of them skips any of the steps we neurons have explained no matter how old they are, what language they speak, or where they live. It takes some humans longer than others, but learning to read, spell, and write is well worth the journey!"

Glossary of Important Terms

Angular Gyrus – This part of the brain helps readers *make meaning from the words they decode* (things, actions, ideas). It is part of the brain where vision, sound, language, and cognition (learning) work together, and is located where the vision, sound, and language parts of the brain meet.

Auditory Cortex – This part of the brain is located in the Temporal Lobe, and has to do with hearing sounds, words, pitch, and even music.

Background Knowledge – This term refers to the information a reader already knows about the world from prior experience or information provided from a book, teacher, parent, and/or caregiver. Increased background knowledge helps readers make sense of the text, improving both reading skill and comprehension.

Brain Hemisphere – The human brain is divided into 2 halves connected by fibers (Corpus Callosum), which send messages to each other. Language and literacy skills typically activate neurons in the left hemisphere.

Broca's Area – This part of the brain is responsible for actual speech production, as well as planning/thinking about what a person wants to say.

Cerebellum – This part of the brain has many functions including: 1-control of voluntary (intended and controlled by people) movements allowing a person to speak, such as opening and closing a person's mouth, as well as eye movements, 2-coordination of muscle movement, balance, and posture, 3-recall in terms of language processing, attention, working memory, and emotional processing, 4-timing muscle actions in terms of reaction time inclusive of procedural learning. All of these functions contribute to the development of a literate brain. The Cerebellum takes up only 10% of the human brain in term of space, but holds more than half of the neurons in a human's brain!

Decode – This term means *reading words*. It is the ability to apply knowledge of sound/letter relationships, knowledge of letter patterns in order to pronounce written words either automatically from previous exposure or to figure out words they have never seen before. Readers should think of decoding as the ability to code from *symbols* to *sounds*.

Encode – This term means *spelling*. It is the ability to apply knowledge of sound/letter relationships, knowledge of letter patterns, and ability to sequence sounds in order to spell words either aloud or in writing. Readers should think of encoding as the ability to code from *sounds* to *symbols*.

Fluency – This term refers to the ability to read accurately (word recognition) with appropriate speed and prosody (with expression) so as to make reading comprehension occur. Another way to think about fluency is to *read like one talks*. All the different types of neurons contribute to a reader's fluency in the following ways:

1. The blue visual neurons work on recognizing words automatically (orthographic mapping).

2. The purple motor neurons work on the eye movements necessary when reading.

3. The green auditory neurons work on decoding unknown words more rapidly as a reader becomes more skilled.

4. The red language neurons work to improve a reader's ability to recognize language patterns in terms of semantics (what word[s] would likely come 'next'), rapid vocabulary recognition, and finally, comprehension.

5. The golden 'Use Your Noodle' neurons work to maintain focus and attention while reading; this is often referred to as 'reading stamina' so that fluent readers can read text closely and for longer periods of time.

Font – This term refers to a set of printed letters with the same design. Examples of fonts are Arial, Helvetica, and Times New Roman.

Frontal Lobe – This part of the brain is located immediately behind the forehead. Its job is to regulate or control behavioral and emotional functions such as attention, judgment, motivation, impulse control, memory, and problem-solving—in other words, executive function skills.

Functional Magnetic Resonance Imaging (fMRI) – This term refers to a way of measuring brain activity by detecting changes in levels of oxygen and blood flow in response to neuronal activities showing which parts of the brain are involved in mental processes. fMRI is a non-invasive (safe) way to measure brain activity.

Grapheme – This term refers to a unit or set of units of a writing system (such as letters and letter combinations) that represent a phoneme (sound) in a written language. Examples include: <t> to represent /t/ and <ch> to represent /ch/, /k/, or /sh/ in English as in "chair," "ache," or "chandelier."

Language – This term refers to a system of agreed-upon spoken, manual (signed), or written symbols. These symbols allow members of a social group of humans to communicate. Human beings are the only species with the inborn ability or the instinct to develop complex oral, spoken language.

Larynx – This is a part of the human vocal mechanism essential to human speech production. During sound production, the vocal cords, located in the larynx, close together and vibrate as air expelled from the lungs passes between them.

CALLING ALL NEURONS!

Literacy – This umbrella term refers to the ability to read (decode), write, spell (encode), listen, and speak with understanding in order to communicate/ share ideas with others.

Metacognition – This term refers to thinking about one's own thinking. It is the ability to pay attention to and monitor the idea of *knowing what you know*, which helps the learning process.

Morphology – This term refers to the smallest unit of meaning in a language. Examples include: -s (suffix <s>) to refer to plural as in *bikes*, present tense verb ending as in *eats*, or possession with the use of an apostrophe as in *girl's* (singular possessive) and *girls'* (plural possessive).

Motor Cortex – This part of the brain is involved in planning, controlling, and executing intended movements, such as making the sounds of speech with the human vocal mechanism, handwriting, eye movements, and pointing to text while reading.

Neuron – This is the basic working unit of the brain. It is a specialized nerve cell, which sends information to other nerve cells, muscles, or gland cells. Many specialized neurons exist, which work together to form a network allowing human beings to read, write, speak, and understand language.

Occipital Lobe – This is a part of the brain involved in visual processes used to store words as images and identify common letter patterns. With exposure and practice, words can be visually accessed automatically without the need to involve the Auditory Cortex.

Orthographic Mapping – This term refers to the cognitive (brain) process humans use to store and retrieve words automatically and effortlessly by connecting their pronunciation (sounds), spelling (letters) and meaning. This term explains how readers read fluently, spell easily, and learn new vocabulary when reading.

HOW READING AND SPELLING HAPPEN

Parietal-Temporal Lobe – This brain area is responsible for a person's ability to connect speech sounds with the visual images of letters. In other words, this area of the brain allows humans to integrate speech sounds with the letters they see when reading. This brain location helps to make meaning of what is read. The Parietal Lobe itself is also responsible for sensory processing including the sensations of touch, pressure, pain, heat, cold, and tension, as well as understanding symbols (written language, numbers, codes, puzzles).

Phoneme – This term refers to the smallest unit of sound in a language. English has ~44 phonemes, depending on dialect (regional differences in pronunciation).

Phonological Awareness – This term refers to the human ability to be aware of oral units of language including words (counting numbers of words in a sentence), syllables, rhymes, and the individual units of sound (phonemes), which are blended together to form words (phonemic awareness). This skill is highly correlated to the development of literacy.

Phonemic Awareness – This term refers to the specific ability to focus upon and manipulate individual speech sounds (phonemes) in spoken words. This skill helps children to connect individual speech sounds to *the actual letters* "matching" the speech sounds and is highly correlated to the development of literacy.

Prefix – This term refers to a single letter or group of letters adding to the meaning of a word placed at the beginning of the word. Examples include: *ex-* (meaning "out") as in *exit* or *exhale* or *in-* (meaning "in") as in *inhale* or *in-* (meaning "not") as in *incomplete*.

Prosody – This term refers to the feature of reading related to reading with expression, phrasing, intonation, and stress patterns. It can be described as the *rhythm* of language when speaking and/or reading.

CALLING ALL NEURONS!

Punctuation – This term refers to the various marks that appear in written text (period, comma, question mark, quotation mark, semicolon, etc.). Punctuation is used to separate sentences and phrases, and it aids meaning, prosody, and fluency.

Retina – The layer at the back of the eyeball sending neurons to the back of the brain where a visual image is formed.

Sound Blending – This term refers to the ability to form words from individual sounds in sequence (order); for example, /b/.../ă/.../t/ = *bat*. This helps new readers decode (read).

Sound Segmentation – This term refers to the ability to hear a word (either from someone or in one's own mind) and separate the word into its individual sounds in sequence (order); for example *bat* = /b/ /ă/ /t/. This helps new readers encode (spell).

Suffix – This term refers to a single letter or group of letters added to the end of the word, which adds meaning to the word. Suffixes have two roles: 1) inflectional, which describes a change in meaning: verb tenses (i.e., *–s* = present tense as in *eats*, -ed = past tense as in *landed*), plural (i.e., -s = plural, 's or s' = possession, -er = comparative as in *bigger, -est* = superlative as in *biggest*; 2) derivational endings that change the "job," "function," "part of speech" of the word (i.e., *–ful* = "full of" as in *wonderful*, -less = "without" as in *helpless*).

Syllable – This term refers to a word or part of a word with a vowel sound, which can be heard, and often it has consonants. It is frequently described as a push of breath (the word *boy* has 1 syllable; the word *fantastic* has 3 syllables). Several consonants are "syllabic"—this means that there is no written vowel, as in the word "rhythm" where the "m" alone produces a syllable.

HOW READING AND SPELLING HAPPEN

Temporal Lobe – This area of the brain includes the Auditory Cortex, which has neurons allowing humans to hear sounds, syllables, words, and sentences, and helps make meaning of language. It is also responsible for naming (of objects, places, people, ideas), development of long-term verbal memory (remembering what has been said), and phonological awareness.

Visual Cortex – This part of the brain is located in the Occipital Lobe, which contains neurons responsible for processing and interpreting visual information sent by the eyes.

Vocabulary – This term refers to all the language and words either used or understood by a person or group of people. Young children experience large growth spurts of vocabulary growth through oral language, whereas older children tend to expand their vocabularies through reading.

Wernicke's Area – This important part of the brain is located in the Temporal Lobe near where the Parietal and Temporal Lobes meet. It is responsible for spoken and written language comprehension.

Word Root – This term refers to a part of a word (or a word on its own—also known as a "base") providing the basic meaning of a word, which can have prefixes, suffixes, or other roots added to it (i.e., *port* = carry as in **trans*port*** and *port**able***, and *struct* = build as in *struct**ure*** and **con*struct***).

The 6 Syllable Patterns in English

CLOSED SYLLABLE – This syllable type is the most common one in English; it appears in about half of all English syllables contained in all English words. A **closed syllable** is a syllable that has *only 1 vowel that is "closed in" by one or more consonants.* The consonants that may or may not appear <u>before</u> the vowel are not considered. If a syllable is "closed," then *the vowel sound is generally* **short**. Examples of closed syllable words are: at, on, it, fish ("sh" closing in the "i;" the "f" is not considered), blast ("st" closing in the "a;" the "b" and "l" are not considered), quit ("t" closing in the "i;" the "qu" is not considered and "u" is not a vowel in this word). *Complete mastery* of the closed syllable concept is important because all the other syllable types are taught <u>in comparison</u> to the closed syllable.

VOWEL-CONSONANT-E SYLLABLE – This syllable type involves the circumstance of a *single vowel, a single consonant, and then an "e" in the final position.* Again, the consonants that may or may not appear <u>before</u> the vowel are not considered. If a syllable follows the V-C-e pattern, then the *first single vowel sound is* **long** *and the* **"e" is silent**. Long "u" is often confusing because it has 2 long sounds: /ū/ as in "cute" and /ü/ as in "flute." Examples of V-C-e syllable words are: ate, eve, Mike (the "M" not considered), home (the "h" not considered), state (the "s" and the "t" not considered).

OPEN SYLLABLE – This syllable type involves the circumstance of *one or more consonants followed by only one vowel <u>without consonants after the vowel</u>.* If a syllable is "open," then *the vowel sound is generally* **long**. The most common way to represent long vowels is the open syllable. The letter "y" may either have the long "i" or long "e" vowel sound in open syllable words. Again, long u is often confusing because it has 2 long vowel sounds: /ü/ as in "flu" and /ū/ as in the first syllable in "unit" (u-nit). Examples of Open Syllable words are: no, I, try, baby (ba-by).

R-CONTROLLED SYLLABLE – This syllable type involves the circumstance of a *single vowel followed by the consonant "r;"* it may or may not have an additional consonant after the vowel. If a syllable is "R-controlled," the vowel sound is **_neither long nor short and is changed by the "r."_** Examples of R-Controlled Syllable words are: car, her, fir, horn, burn, artist (art-ist), corner (cor-ner).

VOWEL TEAM SYLLABLE – This syllable type involves the circumstance of *two vowels next to each other*; consonants may appear either before or after the 2 vowels. If a syllable is a "Vowel Team," the vowel sound may be **_long or short or be part of a slide of 2 different vowel sounds (diphthong)_**. Examples of Vowel Team Syllable words are: each ("ea" = long e), bread ("ea" = short e), boat ("oa' = long o), blue ("ue" = long u as in "flu"), oil ("oi" = diphthong slide combining long o and long e), stray ("ay" = long a), etc.

CONSONANT-LE SYLLABLE – This syllable type involves the circumstance of a multi-syllable word; it is the final syllable in a two- or three-syllable word in most cases. The final syllable follows the pattern of a *single consonant followed by the letters "le" (-Cle)*. If a syllable follows the "C-le" pattern, the **_"e" is silent and the vowel sound is neither long nor short; it has a barely perceptible /uh/ sound between the final consonant and the "l."_** Examples of C-le Syllable words are: little ("tle" = /tŭl/), candle ("dle" = /dŭl/), stable ("ble" = /bŭl/), and example ("ple = /pŭl/).

Additional Notes

1. Why learn the Syllable Patterns? Learning the Syllable Patterns is the "key to the castle" in terms of decoding since recognizing a syllable type will help a reader *determine the vowel sound* in each syllable; this is a major "key" to unlocking many unknown words. Nearly 75 percent of all English syllables are closed or open syllables, with a higher prevalence of closed syllables.

2. Please do <u>not</u> attempt to teach these syllable patterns at one time since it will likely cause the student what is called cognitive over-load. The sequence outlined on pages 86 and 87 provides a good sequence to follow in terms of teaching.

3. It is easier for students to learn the short/long/slide vowel combinations when taught using a keyword with a picture (i.e., "a" apple /ă/ or /ă/ apple "a") in 2 directions, as well as letter formations.

4. You can find a downloadable handout of the *Most Frequent Prefixes and Suffixes in Printed Academic English*. Just scan the QR code and you will see that 51% of all words with prefixes contain only these 3 prefixes: un-, re-, in- (other forms include im-, ir-, il-). You will also see that 65% of all words with suffixes contain only these 3 suffixes: -s (-es), -ed, -ing. Have a look.

5. The information in this book is gleaned from numerous resources, inclusive of books, articles, podcasts, seminars, webinars, personal conversations, etc. Most, if not all, are listed on the My Favorite Resources page of my website. Please feel free to ask questions and/or add comments on my website page.

Acknowledgments

Getting a book into the hands of the intended audience was more difficult than I could ever have imagined, but equally as rewarding now that it is a reality. I want to express my sincere gratitude and appreciation to all my cheerleaders who helped make my dream a reality.

Sincere thanks to my collegial teammates, including Amy Brewer, Ellen Brick, Karen Dakin, Paula Deal, Joyce Hedrick, Donna Hejtmanek, Kelly Hibbler, Karen Keller, Emily Laidlaw, Dr. Kelly Moran, Ambor Moy, Dr. Rebecca Tolson, and Gretchen Walsh. These literacy experts, also champions of the Science of Reading initiative (https://www.thereadingleague.org), took the time to read several versions of my manuscript, offer specific suggestions, challenge me with questions, review illustrations, and patiently support my mission to bring the knowledge of how the human brain learns to read and spell to youngsters. Think about it. It is the youngsters themselves, including my former students Ashley Yarbrough and Jordyn Ruppelli (who also read my manuscript and offered suggestions), the biggest stakeholders in terms of achieving literacy, who need to know this information. After all, understanding the process of attaining literacy serves as a metacognitive and motivational driver for children, all of whom begin school with a desire to learn to read and spell. A special "thank you" to author Denise Eide, as she was able to point me in the right direction when I most needed guidance.

Kudos to my technical support team, including my editor David Aretha, illustrator Jamie Sale, and web designer Brett Hibbler. I want to especially thank David Aretha for leading me to Book Designer Becky Bayne, who is my hero. These professionals tirelessly guided me so that I could express my thoughts most clearly using both words and images. No matter how many Zoom meetings, telephone calls and emails it took, they were always there for me and worked hard to make each aspect of the book creation experience successful.

CALLING ALL NEURONS!

I would be remiss if I did not give a loud shout out to the brain science and literacy giants who inspired me to write this book so that the children who are in the midst of learning how to read and spell know how it is that the lines and squiggles representing speech sounds can be translated to thought. My most sincere admiration and appreciation for your dedication, experience, knowledge base, research, and writing goes to Drs. Stanislaus Dehaene, Louisa Moats, Mark Seidenberg, and Maryanne Wolf. These individuals served as my guiding lights when working for many years with numerous teachers, school administrators, students, and families.

Finally, a big 'hats off' to my family for their unwavering support of my life's work. My husband Dr. Richard Josephson, truly a life partner in every sense, strongly urged me to work on and complete this project. He has been and continues to be a role model who fuels my curiosity, passion, and knowledge base. Watching him interact with his colleagues and patients in his area of expertise has been and continues to be a great influence on mine. My three now adult children, Emily Josephson Black, Adam, and Mitchell Josephson, often waited patiently for me to finish working with one of my many students before attending to their needs. They, too, have encouraged me, and every now and then, offered some technical and emotional support along the winding road of bringing one's thoughts to others in the form of this book.

The ancient African proverb, "It takes a village" is most certainly true. Many thanks and wishes for good fortune to those in my village.

About the Author

Lori Josephson is a Dyslexia Specialist/Educational Consultant who is Fellow of the Orton-Gillingham Academy and holds a Master's Degree in Special Education-Learning Disabilities. She has had the privilege of teaching hundreds of struggling students how to make sense of print and text. She has also had the honor of working with thousands of teachers training them how to teach and reach their students using methods based upon the complex brain processes involved in attaining literacy, the body of knowledge now referred to as the Science of Reading.

Happy Hummingbird
PRESS

https://www.LoriJosephson.com